Illustrated

American Idioms

Acid Test

a test in which findings are beyond any dispute

Example: "Ralph said he could beat me in a one-on-one basketball game. Tonight we're going to play. That will be the *acid test*."

G. JACKMAN

Against All Odds

this idiom describes when there is very little chance or likelihood or probability of success

Example: "We have all heard the story of the Tortoise and the Hare. The very quick Hare should have won the race easily (but he stopped to take a rest). However, *against all odds* the very slow Tortoise persisted at his own steady pace to go on to victory!"

Against The Wind

to struggle and persevere against heavy odds and opposition (as when a sailing ship makes difficult progress, when heading into the wind)

Example: "We were butting our heads, against the city administration, to get our land zoned for farming. We were running *against the wind*!"

Boozed Up

a slang term for being drunk from alcohol (also known as "tanked", "plastered", "stiff", "three sheets to the wind" and "smashed")

Example: "Those people coming out of the beer parlor are really *boozed up*!"

G. JACKMAN

All Ears

to be very interested in hearing all the details about something

Example: "Alfred was *all ears*, when Charlie started talking about what happened, when the police came to the neighborhood last night!"

All In A Day's Work

nothing very special or extraordinary

Example: "The custodian at our school doesn't get angry at the cafeteria clean-up jobs. To him, they are *all in a day's work*!"

All Keyed Up

nervous, tense, excited, hyperactive

Example: "That new baby formula has got the baby *all keyed up*. I think it must have a lot of sugar in it!"

All One's Ducks In A Row

to have everything in your life in the proper order

Example: "Rudy is so darn organized. He always has *all his ducks in a row* !"

All Riled Up

to become wildly annoyed.....extremely upset

Example: "When Phil stepped onto that fresh dog poo down at the park this morning, he was *all riled up*!"

All Thumbs

to be very clumsy

Example: "Ruth dropped a case of those fragile crystal wine glasses. The new manager was so upset. He didn't know that Ruth was *all thumbs*!"

An Old Fogey

a term used to describe an older person who acts in an unsocial or antisocial manner

Example: "Old Mr. Wilson is such a crabby person. He is so antisocial and mean. It's no wonder why people call him *an old fogey!*"

Ants In One's Pants

to be very fidgety....squirmy....restless

Example: "Bill has been so nervous lately. He acts like he has *ants in his pants*!"

G. JACKMAN

As Easy As Pie

      this American Idiom is used to describe whenever something looks like very little work. It is like the expression "This should be a piece of cake."

      Example: "Billy thought this job would be *as easy as pie* to quote; a real piece of cake!"

As Nutty As A Fruit Cake

to say and do things that are crazy

Example: "Norman went out, in the sub zero weather this morning, to shovel snow. He wore nothing but his sandals and a bathing suit. His neighbors think that he is *as nutty as a fruit cake*!"

At A Loss

to be confused

Example: "Mary is *at a loss*, over her best friend's discourteous treatment of her, at the shopping mall last night!"

G. JACKMAN

At The Drop Of A Dime

someone will do something instantly, without any hesitation or thought

Example: "Ronnie loves to play pool so much, that he will join in a money game *at the drop of a dime*!"

At The End Of One's Rope

this idiom refers to a person who is at the limit of their ability, endurance, or patience to do something

Example: "Your sister is *at the end of her rope* with those contraptions she bought to do her hair. The Magic No Hands Mirror keeps slipping, and the Do It Yourself Hair Kit is impossible to understand!"

To Be Back In The Swing Again

      this idiom describes a return to (and to become re-accustomed to) something that you haven't done for a long time......(also known as "to be back in the saddle again)

      Example: "Felicia has been out of school for six weeks. Hopefully, it won't be very long before she returns. I'm sure that she will **be back in the swing of things again**!!"

Back Talk

to reply rudely and quickly to something that someone says

Example: "Jake, that wasn't so smart to give the school nurse all that *back talk*, when she told you to return to the classroom! Now we're going to have deal with the principal!"

A Bad Apple

someone who continuously makes poor choices; mostly anti-social (also known as "a bad penny"...."a bad egg".... " a bad actor")

Example: "I'm worried about your daughter's choice in the company she keeps! Mac Macintosh is *a bad apple*. He's a bad influence!"

A Bad Influence

someone who encourages wrong actions and/or thoughts by their poor examples (also known as "a bad apple"...."a bad egg"...." a bad actor")

Example: "Pete, the pot smoker, is a bad example to the younger kids at our school. He is leading them down a rocky road, by his poor example and illegal choices. He's *a bad influence* for all of the youngsters!

Bad To The Bone

thoroughly and completely bad and evil
....immoral, wicked, dangerous and unlawful
....irredeemable

Example: "Did you see that cranky old man walking around the park today? He actually swatted a little cat with his cane! Anyone that could do something like that is *bad to the bone*."

Bait And Switch

a deceptive merchandising practice, where one product is advertised to get people's attention, but the customer is "hooked" to purchase a different (more expensive) model or item

Example: "Jayne went to the mall to buy a dress that was advertised to sell for $49.00. When she got to the store, the clerk told her that there were no more of that style left. He offered her another dress, that was similar, but more expensive. Jayne was angry at the *bait and switch* sales tactic!"

Baker's Dozen

this idiom refers to bakers who bake thirteen (instead of twelve) for any item that they sell....this practice is to please the customer

Example: "Larry (age six) and his sister Diane (age seven) would always stop by Leighton's bakery to ask if they could have any broken sweets. The baker's helper would smile and give them each a free cupcake! (He always baked a *baker's dozen* anyways!")

Bar Fly

someone who spends too much of his (or her) time in barrooms

Example: "Louie has been drinking since he was twelve. He's been married five times. He spends most of his time with his **bar fly** buddies down at the Golden Banana lounge!

A Barnburner

an American idiom that is used to describe an exciting event (where there is a lot of fast-paced action)

Example: "That basketball play-off game, last night, turned out to be a real *barnburner*!"

A Barrel Of Laughs

someone who is a source of abundant enjoyment....a person who is a great teller of jokes... someone who makes you feel happy through their good humor

Example: "That little Georgie Carlin is so funny at school. He's always a *barrel of laughs* when he makes fun of the teachers. He doesn't care if he gets detentions or not!

A Basket Case

used to describe something (or someone) that is discombobulated and all in pieces…..a person who is a nervous wreck

Example: "Joseph is a stay-at-home dad these days. He is *a real basket case* half of the time!"

To Be Blue

to be deeply sad or in a depressed mood....(also known as "to be down" or "in a funk")

Example: "Jake *is really blue* over the loss of his late wife, Rita!"

A Beer Belly

a fat stomach that protrudes out over the pants that comes from drinking too much beer

Example: "Jake's drinking a six pack every night of the week has presented him with a new problem. Now he is sporting around town with a *beer belly*!"

Behind One's Back

something said or done in one's absence or without one's knowledge (also known as "being sneaky")

Example: "Little Georgie was mocking Mr. Jones in the Math class today. He made faces ***behind the teacher's back*** and, did a drawing on the white board!"

A Bite At The Cherry

this idiom describes an opportunity or chance to do something that you've wanted to do

Example: "Finally, after all this time, I got *a bite of the cherry*! I have been waiting for this since I was ten years old."

A Boatload

an indefinitely large number (or large amount of anything).....extreme abundance or excess

Example: "Farmer Jones needed *a boatload* of chemicals to save his crop this year. I wonder if he'll still sell it as organic produce?

Book Worm

a person who always has their nose buried in a book

Example: "Mr. Jacobs even takes his infant granddaughter to the library. He loves reading books so much. He is such a *book worm*!"

Booze

a slang term for alcohol

Example: "Our neighbors brought a lot of *booze* to the party. We need to keep an eye on those under 21! They are not supposed to have any alcohol."

The Bottom Of The Barrel

this idiom is used to describe any situation when the choices that are left are all of low quality

Example: "We wanted to buy a great tree this Christmas, but by the time we went to cut it down there were hardly any left. We found a tree in the last row that was damaged (but useable). It was *a bottom of the barrel* choice!

Bought The Farm

to die...(also known as "to kick the bucket", "to bite the dust", "to go to the last round-up", and "to pass on")

Example: "Big Albert isn't with us any longer. He *bought the farm* the other day!"

Brain Freeze

this idiom describes two types of brain freeze:
1.) temporary amnesia, also known as "a senior moment" (when you forget the name of a friend)
2.) the splitting headache that happens when you eat ice cream or drink an ice cold beverage

Example: "Justine just drank a large ice-cold milk shake without stopping! She immediately felt a terrible headache that lasted for a couple of minutes! She tried to find the car but she couldn't remember where she parked it. Now that's what's called a real *brain freeze*!)

G.JACKMAN

Bread And Butter

    this idiom refers to the things that are the most important.....those things that are essential in order to have a happy life-style

    Example: "Having a home on the beach is the *bread and butter* of Harry (a salt water fisherman) and his wife, Janie (who loves to paint scenery!)"

Breathe Easier

to feel more secure and at rest....relatively free from worry

Example: "After Steve went to the doctor, and found out that it was cat hairs causing the red spots on his face, he was so relieved. He could *breathe easier*. He was given a tube of topical cream to treat his face."

Bring Home The Bacon

to earn enough income to support a family

Example: "Mike is the bread winner in this house. He's the one who *brings home the bacon*!"

To Be
Broken-Hearted

     this idiom describes a sudden feeling of unhappiness….(also known as "having a heavy heart")…..weighed down by deep sadness

     Example: "Betty was broken-hearted when she found out that her grandparents couldn't make it to her graduation."

Brown Nose

a derogatory term used to describe someone who tries too hard to please someone in a position of authority, in a way that other people find unpleasant…….(also known as "a kiss ass")

Example: "It is so annoying to see James with the boss all the time; saying exactly what the boss wants to hear. He is a genuine **brown nose**!

Bubbly

an idiom that means "full of life", "bouncy", "animated", "lively"

Example: "When Elly showed up for the party, everyone gathered around her, as if she were a magnet! She is so *bubbly*!"

Buckle Down

an American idiom that is used to describe whenever a person applies himself (or herself) with determination to work hard, with full attention to details

Example: "Charlie and Bob **buckled down** to the job of rebuilding the antique bus seat to the best of their abilities."

Bump Into

a chance meeting with someone that you haven't seen in a long while

Example: "I *bumped into* Sally Jones today. She was Christmas shopping, down town, in Newburyport!"

A Bun In The Oven

this idiom refers to a woman who is pregnant (also called "with child", "expecting", "in a family way", and/or eating for two")

Example: "I saw that your granddaughter, Elizabeth has *a bun in the oven*. She told me that her husband and she have been trying for the past year. They feel so blessed. The doctor thought that there might be twins!"

A Bundle Of Nerves

a term used to describe a person who is extremely nervous and fit to be tied because of their behavior

Example: "They had to take the clerk at CVS to the hospital this afternoon. An angry customer was so upset, that he had mistakenly sold her nerve medication to some other customer, that she over reacted. She was *a bundle of nerves* and very irate!"

Buried

an expression used when someone has been given too much work to do

Example: "Rodney can't get to your automobile right now. He has 14 other cars to repair today. *He is buried* !"

Burned

to pay too much for something....to purchase anything, and get much less than what you paid for....to pay a high price for a low quality product

Example: "I really got *burned* when I bought that television for Electrode City. It doesn't pick up half the stations that my old television did!"

Burst Someone's Bubble

to destroy someone's illusion or their fantasy

Example: "I hate to burst your bubble, but you will never make it to Vegas on those old tires!"

Bury One's Head In The Sand

      a term used to describe when a person ignores something that is obviously wrong (not facing the reality of a situation)

      Example: Donald Trump lives in another world. He ignores truth, tells lies, and misleads his loyal followers! He is expert in knowing how to *bury his head in the sand*."

Busting Butt

working very hard....achieving above and
beyond what is normally accomplished

Example: "Ludwig was *busting his butt*
when digging that trench this morning!"

Busy As A Beaver

very busy getting things done... hard-working.... productive

Example: "Ludwig is so industrious. It's no wonder that he gets things done. He is always as *busy as a beaver*!"

Buy It For A Song

to purchase something for very little money
…(also known as "to get a great deal" or "a steal")

Example: "Did you see the bike Al picked up?
Yes I did. *I heard he bought it for a song*
too!

A Cake Walk

this idiom is used to describe an easy victory......a one-sided contest......(synonym for "a piece of cake")

Example: "That football game on T.V last night was so lopsided!" It was *a cake walk* for the winners; a real piece of cake!"

G.JACKMAN

Can't Hold A Candle
to Someone

unable to reach someone else's level when compared

Example: "Alfred is always being compared to his older brother. It's very unfortunate that he **can't hold a candle to him**."

Carry The Ball

to take major responsibility for an organization's undertaking

Example: "Bob was given the collection department's two major accounts. The President is asking him to *carry the ball*!"

Carved In Stone

this idiom refers to something that can't be changed
in any way....it is permanent and unalterable

Example: "That rock that they call 'The Old Man Of
The Mountain' has been there for many, many
years. It is *carved in stone*. It is one of America's
natural beauties!"

Cash On The Barrelhead

this American Idiom is used to describe whenever complete payment is required for an item at the time of the purchase.....no credit extended .....no haggling or bargaining.....cash only

Example: "Mary Anne sold her Vincent Black Lightning motorcycle for fifty thousand dollars *cash on the barrelhead*!"

Castle In The Sky

     this idiom refers to dreams, hopes, or plans that are unrealistic and that have very little chance of succeeding......imagining unachievable daydreams

     Example: "Bill is out in the back yard daydreaming, instead of bagging leaves! There's nothing wrong with building *castles in the sky*, just as long as you work hard to set them on strong foundations here on earth !"

A Cat On A Hot Tin Roof

to be nervous and uncomfortable and not able to keep still

Example: "I don't see Ben fidgety very often. Today he is acting like *a cat on a hot tin roof*!"

Catch Some Z's

to get some sleep….to take a nap…(also known as "catch 40 winks" or "get some shut eye")

Example: "Jim was so tired from working in the hay fields, that he *caught some z's* during the afternoon break!"

Caught Red-Handed

this idiom means that someone is caught in the middle of committing a crime....or breaking the law

Example: "Johnny Cain was *caught red-handed* by the police yesterday. He became a suspect when they saw all the blood on his hands, and his friend Billy Bob was on the ground, with a knife sticking out of his chest!"

Chameleon

this idiom refers to a person who changes his (or her) beliefs or behaviors in order to succeed.....the chameleon lizard has the unique ability to change colors so that it can blend into the environment and be safe from predators or any other danger

Example: "Ron is a political *chameleon*. He will swing vote and change his mind at the drop of a dime; (Just as long it helps him to succeed) !"

Chip Off The Old Block

     this idiom describes an individual who is just like one of their parents in character or behavior

     Example: "Little Doug reminds me of his father. Everything he says or does; even the way he dresses! He is a real *chip off the old block* !"

Close Call

something bad that almost happened (also known as a "close shave")

Example: "That was a *close call* this morning, when Olivia and Tom were talking on their phones. A piano fell from the 6th floor and just missed them!"

To Come Out Of The Closet

this American Idiom is used to describe whenever someone publicly announces a belief or preference that one has kept hidden

Example: "Billy Bob told his family that he supported Gay Rights. He *came out of the closet* with his secret. His family, who were all against that movement were shocked!"

Cooking The Books

presenting false documents (that show less profits or more profits)....making false entries (to make a business better than it actually is)

Example: "Bernie Madoff stole from thousands of investors and made millions of dollars in profits when he falsified investment information. He really ***cooked the books*****!**"

Cool As A Cucumber

to be calm and relaxed when in a stressful situation

Example: "Art never appears nervous. He always stays calm. He stays as cool as a cucumber!"

G JACKMAN

Cry Over Spilt Milk

this idiom means that it is a waste of time to get upset and angry over any situation that has already happened and can not be changed

Example: "Aunt Bertha was so teary-eyed, when her little cat felix reached up onto the kitchen table, and knocked the half gallon of milk all over the place. I guess you could say that she was *crying over spilt milk*."

Cutting Corners

this idiom describes whenever a person is doing a task too quickly and does not worry about the details.....resulting in a job poorly done and half completed

Example: "Billy Bean rushed through is cleaning chore last Saturday. His mother checked his work and became angry when she found dirt and dust over half of the room. When he got home for supper, she told him that he was grounded for a week; that no one in her family would be allowed to *cut corners* like that."

Daily Grind

this idiom is used to describe anyone's daily work routine (especially when it is tiresome and tedious)

Example: "Charlie and Bob go about their daily grind without complaint. They know that it is hard work, but somebody has to do it!"

To Dance Around

this idiom describes whenever a person is purposefully avoiding something

Example: "Doug didn't mention the cost of the new motorcycle that he had purchased. He kept avoiding his wife's questions. He continued *dancing around*, hoping that she would start talking about something else!"

Dead End

this American idiom describes whenever a path or situation leads to nowhere or offers no prospects

Example: "Felicia saw that the job she had taken was a real dead end. All the promises that were made to her never materialized. She decided to hand in her notice; and start looking for a job with greater opportunities!"

Deep Water

to be in a difficult situation which is hard to deal with or impossible to manage (also known as "in over one's head")

Example: "When William switched into the Latin IV class, he got himself in *deep water*! Now his other classes are suffering."

Die With Their Boots On

this idiom is used to describe anyone who is so happy with the way they make a living that they don't ever want to retire.......they just want to die on the job

Example: "John loves his vocation! Every morning he starts off with a smile and thanks God for the blessings! He reminds me of the old western Desperados (who were always waiting for another train to rob!) They all wanted to *die with their boots on*."

A Drop In The Bucket

not too important because it doesn't amount to much

Example: "I'm not worried about the taxes on that new beach home we just bought. I'm loaded. To me, those taxes won't amount to *a drop in the bucket!"*

The Early Bird Catches The Worm

rise early in the morning and get to work before others and you will have a better chance at success

Example: "Bill is always up at 4 a.m.. He believes that *the early bird catches the worm*!"

Egg Head

this idiom is used to describe anyone who is a genuine intellectual or genius

Example: "Paul worked for FDR, back in the days of the WPA. He was one of the original *egg heads* that President Roosevelt surrounded himself with."

Have Egg On Your Face

       this idiom is used to describe when a person is embarrassed and feels foolish (because something that he had done in the past becomes common knowledge and it has come back to haunt him)

       Example: "Jerry predicted that something like this would never happen in his town. Now his friends are reminding him; they've made sure that he *has egg on his face* now!"

Elbow Grease

this idiom is used to describe whenever someone needs to work harder at their manual labor

Example: "Charlie and Bob have always been a hard-working team. Both know when a little more elbow grease is needed to meet deadlines."

Every Cloud Has A Silver Lining

this idiom means that there is something good in every bad situation....it is an expression of hope

Example: "That dark cloud has put Wilbur in a depressed state. John Milton would say that there is a bright sunshine behind that dark cloud, and that *every cloud has a silver lining* !"

To Eye Something

to give a closer look at something of interest

Example: "When the mayor *eyed* the job offer in the next city over, rumors started that he was leaving our city for a better paying job!"

Fair-Weather Friends

this idiom describes people who are your friends only in the good times.....they will be hard to find when times get rough and the weather gets stormy

Example: "Pete had a slew of friends until his accident. Now he can't find any of them. *Fair-weather friends* desert you. A true friend will always be there for you."

this American idiom describes whenever a person is missed, overlocked, or mistakenly left out

   Example: "Someone forgot to include the new kids that just moved into town! We can't just let them *fall through the cracks* like that!"

Feeding-Frenzy

this idiom describes an out of control eating behavior that one can witness when piranha fish swarm to eat a chunk of flesh thrown into water

Example: "The chipmunks at Calvin's house had a **feeding-frenzy** on the wires of his new van. It cost him a small fortune to replace those wires (not to mention the tow charge!)"

Fiddle Around

to play with something.....to tinker with something ineptly

Example: "Old Joe Clark is out back *fiddling around* with your lawn mower engine. It may never run again!"

G. JACKMAN

Fly By Night

not reliable or responsible (especially in business).....untrustworthy.....not lasting.....impermanent.....transitory

Example: "Allen was upset that the company who sold and installed his new window (with a lifetime warranty) had left town, without leaving a forwarding address, and their phone had been disconnected. He learned too late that the company was a *fly by night* operation!"

To Fly Off The Handle

to behave like a crazy person who loses his (or her) temper suddenly and unexpectedly……to fly into a rage…..to explode because of something said or what someone did or did not do

Example: "When Jerry saw Maryanne with Bruce, He was so mad he *flew off the handle*!"

A Fly On The Wall

     this idiom means that you would like to secretly hear what is being said.....or see what will happen (while not being noticed)

     Example: "I would love to *be a fly on the wall* in the main office tomorrow when they find out who left the lights on all night."

this idiom is used to show when someone becomes overly excited or involved and takes things too far

Example: "Charlie is so happy to have found the sticking power of duct tape, that he uses it to fix everything. I think he gets carried away sometimes."

Get Off One's Back

to stop nagging, irritating, bothering, harassing, irking

Example: "Big Bill wouldn't stop pestering Betty about her sudden weight gain. He wouldn't *get off her back* about it!"

To Get The Green Light

to be given the go ahead sign....to be given permission to do something (also known as "to be given the nod")

Example: "Alfred has been waiting for weeks, for permission to build that deck off the back of his cottage. Finally, the commission has *given him the green light*!"

Get Your Goat

this idiom means to annoy someone very badly…to make a person very angry….red under the color angry

Example: "Did you see that move that Jimmy put on the other team's point guard? That's the third time Jimmy stole the ball from him! Their point guard is so angry. Jimmy has got his number. He also has *got his goat* !"

Go Ballistic

this American idiom describes whenever a person shows extreme anger and acts out (in a vengeful way) without mercy or thought

Example: "Big Jake was so angry about the missing trees from his tree farm that he *went ballistic*."

To Go Bonkers

to become wild, restless, and unruly....crazy
.....irrational.......to lose one's sanity

Example: "When dad comes home and finds out you wrecked the family car, he will surely *go bonkers*!"

G. JACKMAN

Good Frame Of Mind

to be in a happy, relaxed, and contented mood

Example: "I have never seen Mortimer so calm and collected. He sure is in a *good frame of mind*!"

Gravy Job

this idiom is used to describe whenever work is easy (and almost fun)......or, any job where someone makes an excessive amount of money without expending much effort

Example: "Luka was enjoying painting the fence with his new spraying machine. The work went so much faster and the payoff was terrific! He wished every job was as easy as this *gravy job*!"

Half Baked

Any action or scheme that hasn't been thought out or planned very well

Example: "Peter wasn't cautious when he was checking on the electrical connections. That was a *half baked* idea!"

Half In The Bag

to be intoxicated (or well on the way)

Example: "Sparky was *half in the bag* when he showed up to rake the yard today!"

A Hard Nut To Crack

a difficult person or thing or problem to deal with

Example: "Those kids in the high school's World Literature class are *hard nuts to crack*!"

Hats Off To You

this idiom is used to express congratulations to someone (out of respect for something they said or did)

Example: "Hats off to you, Jesse! I didn't think someone your age would even know who that guitar player was."

Have A Blast

to have a great time doing something that you enjoy.....to have a lot of fun

Example: "Brenda and Joanne *had a blast* at you party last night."

To Have A Lot Of Balls

to have a lot of nerve and gumption….a lot of testosterone (assertive and aggressive ways of behaving)

Example: "*You've got a lot of balls* coming in here and accusing me of stealing your favorite fishing spot!"

A Run-In With The Law

this idiom describes whenever someone gets into serious trouble with the police

Example: "The cops chased Billy through seven towns, before they were able to stop him. The State Troopers set up a road block that popped all of Billy's brand new tires. This is not the first time that he has had *a run-in with the law*. He will lose his license to for a full year, because of this stunt!"

G. JACKMAN

To Have Moxie

to have guts or courage

Example: "Mr. Jones really *has a lot of moxie* to speak up to the president of his company like that. He will be lucky if he isn't fired. Nobody dares to talk back to the president!"

To Have The World
By The Tail

     to have everything go exactly the way you want it to go …..to be successful and happy at whatever your calling is in life

     Example: "Holly is so lucky. Everything is going so well for her. It's no wonder that she thinks she *has the world by the tail*!"

Having A Bone To Pick

to have a grievance with someone that needs to be talked about

Example: "Joseph is really angry with the way Tom took over the building plan, at last night's meeting. He told me he *has a bone to pick* with Tom this morning, when we meet for coffee!"

Hissy Fit

this idiom is used to describe whenever a person is having a temper tantrum (also known as "a meltdown", "a rant", "an emotional outburst") that typically ends up in physically violent behavior

Example: "When Marion found out about her husband's involvement with another woman, she went into a real *hissy fit*!"

G. JACKMAN

Hot Off The Press

a term used to describe a freshly-printed book or paper....used also to describe anything that has just been newly made or manufactured

Example: "I'm reading the latest book about American Education. *It's hot off the press*!"

Hot Rodding

a term used to describe speeding, peeling rubber, jack rabbit starts, racing and otherwise disobeying the traffic laws

Example: "Billy's in trouble with the law, again. This morning he was caught *hot rodding* down Main Street by officer Crabby!"

If The Shoe Fits, Wear It

if someone uses this idiom when talking to you, they are telling you that any unpleasant remarks which have been made about you are most likely true

Example: "Jimbo told Allen that he was a busybody. Allen told Ellen what Jimbo said. Ellen told Allen "*If the shoe fits, wear it*!""

G. JACKMAN

In Full Swing

to recover quickly from sickness….to get back to the healthy condition that you were in before

Example: "That new bridge that they are building from Newburyport to Salisbury is *in full swing*. That old bridge was a hazard to travelers!"

In One Ear & Out The Other

     this American idiom describes when something is heard but is completely forgotten

     Example: "The cook made the super but forgot that you cannot have salt! I think that my talk with him yesterday must have gone *in one ear and out the other*."

In The Dog House

to get punished for a poor choice or behavior, by being locked out of a home by a spouse

Example: "Peter forgot that it was his wife's birthday. He will be in the *dog house* now!"

It Takes Two To Tango

       this idiom suggests that certain actions or activities cannot be performed alone; two people must participate and, both people involved in the situation are equally responsible

       Example: "We both bought that car together. You can't keep blaming me every time it breaks down! You're just as responsible for the poor choice as I am. Don't forget, *it takes two to tango*!"

Joined At The Hip

to be exceptionally close to another
......seemingly inseparable

Example: "Bill and Bob were twin brothers who did everything together. Their wives would often tell them, in jest, that they were *joined at the hip*!

Jump Down Someone's Throat

to talk or scream at someone in a very angry and unpleasant, out of control manner

Example: "Alice was so angry with the store clerk (for not having the merchandise that she had put on hold) that *she jumped down his throat*"!

Jump Start

to get going in the morning (with a cup of coffee) when you are very tired and unmotivated

Example: "Last night's overtime was exhausting. I could barely keep my eyes open this morning. I needed a *jump start* to get up and running!"

Jump The Gun

to do or say something before you should have

Example: "Alexander moved quickly on the purchase of that new automobile. Bank rates went down this week. He could have saved a bundle if he had waited. His impatience caused him to *jump the gun*!"

Keep Cool

to stay calm during unnerving situations

Example: "I don't know how our Science teacher stays so calm, when the students are acting up! How can someone *keep cool* in such situations?"

Keep Your Eye On The Ball

to give your undivided attention to what you are doing all the time….to stay focused on something

Example: "Glenda is such a great book keeper. Her attention to the numbers is exceptional. She really does *keep her eye on the ball*!"

Keep Your Nose To
The Grindstone

to work very hard at a particular task or job.....
staying focused and intent.....paying close attention to
details

Example: "Jimmy's boss is happy when his workers
keep their nose to the grindstone."

Keep One's Shirt On

to be patient....not so quick to jump into a fight or an argument

Example: "Hey Bud! *Keep your shirt on*! His statement wasn't directed at you!"

to relax.....to take it easy.....to take a break from a routine....to rest...to take a load off your feet

Example: "Jake had just worked a 12 hour shift watching over a sick friend. He felt that he deserved to kick back for a while!"

Grand Slam

in American baseball a grand slam occurs when a batter hits a home run with the bases loaded, thereby scoring four runs

    Example: "Big Bob hit a *grand slam* when he landed a contract with a million dollar company. He knows how to wheel and deal for sure."

To Laugh All The Way
To The Bank

this idiom describes persons who make a lot of easy profit by exploiting other peoples necessities

Example: "The prices of our gas and oil have climbed tenfold since we were kids! Those greedy oil companies must be *laughing all the way to the banks*! "

To Let The Genie Out Of The Bottle

something has happened which has made a great and permanent change in peoples' lives (especially a bad change)

Example: "This pandemic has been a plague upon humanity! It's like germ warfare! Somehow *the genie has been let out of the bottle*!!!"

A Little Bird Told Me

information learned from a mysterious or secret source….(also known as "I heard it through the grapevine")

Example: "Who told you that story about Richard?" '*A Little Bird Told Me*!' "

To Make A Long Story Short

this idiom describes whenever a person is telling a story, and they should be skipping a lot of unnecessary details (because they see that people that they are talking to are losing their interest)

Example: "Jake's stories are way too long! He should know by now that he needs *to make his long stories short*, or he'll lose his audience."

To Make A Nuisance Of One's Self

to be a constant bother to somebody..(also known as "to be a pain in the neck")

Example: "Those chipmunks in Joseph's backyard are *making a nuisance of themselves*. Just last week, they chewed all the wires out of his van. Now, they done it again!"

G.JACKMAN

Mixed Feelings

feeling negative and positive, sad and happy at the same time

Example: "Bill was at Shaw's market, looking for his favorite snack. He couldn't find it displayed anywhere. He asked one of the stocking clerks if she knew where it was. She told him that he could find it at the Demoulas market that was next door. Bill thanked her. But as he walked out of the store, he wondered if that helpful and courteous clerk had *mixed feelings* about giving him that information about a competitor!"

Need More Elbow Room

a need for less restrictions.......more room to grow
more freedom.....more space

Example: "Carl says that he doesn't need someone
hovering over him. He says that he needs more *elbow
room*!"

A Nest Egg

an amount of money that has been put away for future use or retirement.....usually kept secretly

Example: "Buddy has been saving 10 percent of his earnings for 65 years. He has only told his wife. He called it their little *nest egg* !"

Nit Wit

a term used do describe someone who is a stupid or silly person (who does not learn from their mistakes)

Example: "Benny seems to be always getting himself into trouble at our school. He just keeps making wrong choices. Some of his classmates think he is a *nit wit*!"

No Brainer

a decision or choice that requires little or no thought (because it is so obvious)

Example: "Jake could pick up the baseball or pick up the gopher. The choice was a *no brainer*!"

On The Fritz

an American idiom that describes whenever something is no longer working properly and out of order

Example: "Seeing Charlie mending everything that is broken, using his favorite duct tape, is like watching a magic trick! He fixes anything that is **on the fritz**!"

Pain In The Ass

someone who does things on purpose that are aggravating, irritating, and mean-spirited

Example: "That snowplow driver waited for twenty minutes at the top of our street, until I finished shoveling the driveway. As soon as I completed the task, and went into the house, he came down the street and added four more feet of snow across the entry of the driveway! Now that's what I call a *pain in the ass*!"

A Plum Assignment

this idiom describes any job that is considered very easy to accomplish and it pays well too

Example: "Jim is the son-in-law of the company's owner. That is why he is always given the biggest *plum assignments*!"

A Pretty Penny

a term used to describe when anything bought is extremely expensive (also known as "it cost an arm and a leg")

Example: "I'll bet that new house Bill bought cost him *a pretty penny*!!"

G.JACKMAN

Red Tape

Large amounts of bureaucratic paperwork that is difficult or impossible to complete and is seemingly pointless

Example: "Peter was extremely agitated at the amount of *red tape* that was a barrier to his getting a Social Security Number."

A Rip Off

this idiom refers to something being too expensive….. to cheat someone by charging them too much money

Example: "The Jones family, before going into the desert, paid ten dollars a gallon for gas, and six dollars for each bottle of water! They felt it was *a rip off*, but they really needed those items."

A Roll In The Hay

this idiom means that someone is involved in a casual sexual encounter (also known as "a roll in the sack")

Example: "Roger skipped school, and went next door for a *roll in the hay* with his newly divorced neighbor!"

To See The Light

to understand something clearly at last

Example: "Tim thought and thought and thought about the problem. After many hours of hard thinking, he finally *saw the light*!"

A Sinking Ship

any company or organization that is doing poorly, in distress, or headed for bankruptcy or closure

Example: "Robert's employer had made some bad management decisions a short while ago. So Rob switched jobs because he felt that the company was *a sinking ship*."

A Slap On The Wrist

this idiom describes whenever someone in authority gives a minor punishment for an anti-social act (when the punishment should be more severe)

Example: "The judge gave Bad Boy Louie *a slap on the wrist*, again. That kid could get away with murder with this judge! The cops don't understand why the judge does not throw the book at him!"

A Snowball In Hell

no chance.....not possible

Example: "I don't think that baseball team has the chance of *a snowball in hell* for winning the title this year. They are terrible."

A Sponge

this American idiom describes someone who asks for money (or other things) from someone else, and makes no effort to pay it back

Example: "Jeffrey is *a sponge*! He's always asking for a loan (that he never pays back)! Why doesn't he ever have any money of his own?"

To Be A Stick In The Mud

this idiom describes any person who is unwilling to participate in an activity......(also known as a "party pooper" or a "curmudgeon")

Example: "Everyone was having a ball at the party this afternoon, with the exception of Bud. He's just an old *stick in the mud*; so old fashioned."

to exaggerate a story…..to tell a story and stretch it way out of proportion…..to say something that is not completely honest…..to make something seem better that it really is

sstretching The Truth   **Example:** "Josh was telling a story about the fish he caught last week. Everyone knew he has a history of *stretching the truth*! No one believed him."

A Tenderfoot

someone who is inexperienced at something.....
new to a task

Example: "Diane just started oil painting as a hobby. She retired, after 40 years of being the best hairdresser in the State! She's *a tenderfoot* at her new art, but she loves it just the same!

The Good Book

The Holy Bible

Example: "William is never seen without *The Good Book* in his hand. He should be a preacher!"

A Junkyard Dog

a term used to describe a person who is so tough that he (or she) is not afraid of anyone or anything….a person who welcomes confrontation

Example: "Joey is so tough, rough, and ready to meet anyone, anywhere, anytime, anyplace in any confrontation. He is absolutely fearless! That's how he got his famous nickname, '*The Junkyard Dog*'!"

Thin Blue Line

this idiom describes the brotherhood of police forces in America

Example: "The police in town are really close to each other They live up to their oaths and they support their community. They also support all other officers all over the State and Country!" It is no wonder why they are called the *thin blue line*."

The Point Of No Return

to be at a point where it is too late to turn back

Example: "Mr. Jones' last thought, before he went over the waterfall at Niagara, must have been that he had reached *the point of no return*."

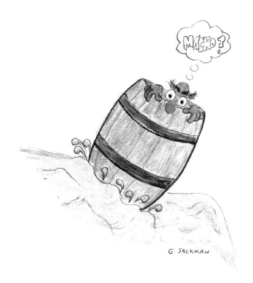

The Tables Are Turned

this idiom describes whenever a situation has changed (especially one that results in the opposite of an earlier situation)

Example: "Wow! Jerry's heavy drinking got him in a lot of trouble, when he showed up at an NAACP rally. ***The tables were turned***, to say the least!"

The Walls Have Ears

to speak very softly, because someone may be listening....the walls may be so thin, that what is said in private, becomes public news

Example: "Danny should be more careful with his opinion. Word will get back to the management, and he will be in deep water! I guess he doesn't know that *the walls have ears*!"

Thinking Out Of The Box

to think creatively to find new solutions to problems......to think freely, not to be bound by old ways of doing things

Example: "Big Eddie couldn't get his bull back into the barn, no matter how hard he pulled! Little Joe grabbed the rope, turned the bull around and pulled so hard. To Big Eddie's surprise, the bull backed himself into the barn! Now that was *thinking out of the box*!!"

A Thorn In One's Side

this idiom is used to describe whenever a person or someone's actions cause a lot of problems for someone else

Example: "Leroy ordered a super-sized piece of frosted cake to eat in front of his poor wife. He knew she was on a weight-watching program (and that she could not eat what he ordered). He was acting to undermine her program. She told me that Leroy was *a thorn in her side*; that she was stronger than that; and that she was not going to let him sabotage her in any way!!"

Through Thick And Thin

this idiom is used to describe whenever someone is there to support another person (no matter how challenging or difficult it might be) through good and bad times

Example: "Bob has been working with Charlie since they were teenagers. Over time, they have stuck together *through thick and thin*. That's why they are such good friends."

Throw A Lifeline

to use one's skills to help someone else who is in trouble

Example: "Jack couldn't make good on the baseball uniforms delivery. Jim stayed to help. The delivery was made, on time, because Jim *threw a lifeline to Jack*!"

Throw The Dog A Bone

to give someone something that will make them happy for a while

Example: "Richard, did you get that report to the boss by 3 p.m.?" "Yes, I gave him an old one that I found in my file drawer. I *threw the dog a bone*!"

Throw Someone Under The Bus

    this idiom is used to describe whenever a person avoids responsibility for a wrong-doing.....instead, they point the figure at someone else (and let them take the blame for the action)

    Example: "Charlie *threw Bill under the bus* when he told Bill's wife that Bill was the reason they got home late last night!"

Tickled Pink

this idiom means to be well pleased....to feel delighted....to be overjoyed

Example: "That Flamingo that we saw yesterday looked very happy eating those little pink krill. I guess you could rightly say that he was *tickled pink* to be where he was."

Time Flies

time passes by so quickly (especially when you are having fun)

Example: "I haven't seen Constantine in a dog's age. Now look at him. He's all grown up!
Time Flies!"

The Tip Of The Iceberg

this idiom means that only part of something can be seen, the rest of it is deep below the water's surface

Example: "Donald thinks this is going to be an easy job. He has no idea that what he is looking at is just *the tip of the iceberg*. There is so much to do that Donald can't see!"

Toast

a slang term that is used to describe a person who is doomed, in trouble, or not worthy of consideration (also used in the computer trades to describe any inoperable system or component .....especially one that has "crashed" or "burned")

Example: "Thelma can kiss that job goodbye, since they found out about her political views. Around here, she is *toast*!"

Toast Of The Town

to be liked and admired by the people who know you (who are from your city or town)

Example: "Harry and Rita were the *toast of the town* when they saved the company and all those jobs!"

Tongue In Cheek

to jokingly tease someone about something

Example: "Jake was making a *tongue in cheek* remark when he told Anna that her looked too curly."

Too Many Chiefs And Not Enough Indians

too many managers and not enough workers to do the required labor to complete the job

Example: "What's going on here? There are five management people and only two workers! At this rate, we'll never meet the deadline! There *are too many chiefs and not enough indians*!"

G. JACKMAN

Too Many Cooks Spoil
The Stew

too much input (or too many contributors to a solution) will cloud the issues, and will lead to further frustration and failure

Example: "Everyone is trying to fix this company's problems, and we're getting nowhere. *Too many cooks spoil the stew!*"

To Toot Your Own Horn

to talk about oneself or one's accomplishments or achievements in a way that shows pride or too much pride

Example: "In an important job interview yesterday, Bradley was *tooting his own horn* telling about all the wonderful things he had done for the company he had last worked for."

Top Banana

a very important person....the most important person in the group, or undertaking ....(also known as "big wig", "heavy hitter", "top gun", and "big cheese")

Example: "Charlie Zimmer is the most influential leader in that organization. He's got a better sales record than any other person. He is their company's *top banana!*"

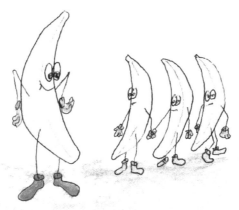

Touch A Sore Spot

to refer to a sensitive matter that will upset someone

Example: "It looks like I *touched a sore spot*, Bill. I'm sorry. I didn't mean to upset you."

G·JACKMAN

Touch And Go

a situation that is uncertain, shaky, unstable, or unsteady (also known as "Not Out Of The Woods Yet")

Example: "Bill's health is failing rapidly, since the accident. Whether or not he will recover at all, is still *touch and go*!"

Tricks Of The Trade

this idiom is used to describe clever methods of getting a job done that are used by people who are experienced in a particular work or activity

Example: "Steve really knows how to remove dents and rust from an automobile. His repainted cars look better than new! He knows a *few tricks of the trade*! Besides that, he charges much less than others!!"

Turn A Blind Eye

whenever any person can see something wrong going on and they pretend not to see anything

Example: "Some lady was taking a picture of her small dog that had climbed a tree down at the riverside park ! She had let the pet of the leash (which was against the law), then called the police to get help ! Now if that isn't *turning a blind eye*, nothing is !"

Two Peas In A Pod

this idiom is used to describe when two people bear a strong resemblance or enjoy the same activities

Example: "Bud and Rockette have been married for 57 years. They have a large family of kids, grandkids, and great grandkids. In many ways they are **two peas in a pod**!

To Undermine

to make someone weaker or less likely to succeed at something that they are trying to accomplish

Example: "Old Mr. McKay is always trying *to undermine* his wife's attempt to lose weight. What is his problem?"

Up The Creek Without A Paddle

to find yourself in a challenging situation, especially one that cannot be easily resolved....also expressed as "up the proverbial creek without a paddle"

Example: "My musician friend Roger was *up the proverbial creek without a paddle* when he found out that he lost his guitars in the fire that his ex-wife set in his house!" Poor Roger made his living with those instruments!!"

Ups And Downs

this idiom describes good times and bad times, successes and failures, life's reciprocity of give and take

Example: "Bud and Rockette have had their share of *ups and downs* over the years. In a large family, that's the way it goes! They will tell you that they are happy to be alive and healthy."

Vegging Out

to spend time idly or passively

Example: "Reggie is in the parlor relaxing and *vegging out*!"

Wait And See

to be patient enough to wait until a later time

Example: "It's out of your control. You will just have to wait and see!"

Waiting In The Wings

to be waiting, ready and prepared to do something when the right time comes along

Example: "Jacob has been eagerly *waiting in the wings* for Paul's early retirement party. He has been the old timer's understudy for a few years. Jacob is sure to be Paul's replacement!"

Walking On Eggs

to be extremely cautious and careful and light-footed

Example: "Joseph is so worried about his wife's blood pressure problem, that he goes throughout the house *walking on eggs*, so that he won't upset her!"

To Wear Many Hats

this idiom comes from the days when craftsmen of different trades wore hats of their trade.....in America today, this is used to describe a person who does a variety of jobs

Example: "Bell is a valuable person at the office. She *wears many hats*, and does everything to perfection!"

Wear Your Heart On Your Sleeve

openly showing your emotions for someone else without intending (to the point where others will take advantage of you)

Example: "Thelma feels sorry for Robert. It's clear, she *wears her heart on her sleeve.*"

When One's Ship Comes In

when someone becomes rich and successful after many years of labor and set-backs

Example: "Paul is just waiting for *his ship to come in*. Things will change for him, when it finally happens!"

When Pigs Fly

a term used to describe a situation that will never happen (also known as "When Hell Freezes Over")

Example: "Robert will be able to throw that football one hundred yards *when pigs fly*!"

G. JACKMAN

White Knuckle Driving

this idiom refers to driving with the hands clutching the steering wheel so tightly (in a state of great tension and fear) that the knuckles turn white

Example: "Bart drives to work every morning going 85 miles per hour. People on the highway are swerving in and out, passing him on the left and right, and talking on their cell phones. Most of his hectic trips are nerve-wracking, *white knuckle driving*."

Wishful Thinking

      believing that something is true or that something will happen because one wishes that it were true or would happen

      Example: "Thinking that Trump will win the election is just *wishful thinking* on your part. You might as well think that you're going to find a wardrobe at the mall for the dance that you will be able to afford!"

Wolf In Sheep's Clothing

this idiom describes whenever a person acts honest, upright, straight-forward, and sincere, but they are just pretending.....they are evil and have bad intentions

Example: "Sally thought William was a great young man. After she married him she found out that he was a *wolf in sheep's clothing*. She had been fooled by a pretender."

Work Up An Appetite

a term used to describe a person who has worked at something so long and hard that they need a bite to eat....in some cases the food of choice is not a healthy one

Example: "Tim had just left the Weight Watcher meeting when, on his way home, he stopped at the ice cream stand to get his favorite chocolate triple-scooper! I guess that meeting caused Tim to *work up an appetite*!"

Working For Peanuts

to work for almost no money….(also known as "chicken feed")

Example: "Steve should quit that job! He's *working for peanuts*, and he'll never get ahead!"

Working Under The Table

to work for pay, without the government knowing, in order to avoid taxes

Example: "Carl is painting houses , *under the table*, on the weekend to help to feed his growing family."

Worm In The Apple

this idiom means that something you thought was a good thing turns out to be bad or spoiled

Example: "Justine bit into that bright red apple and found out that it was rotten…filled with worms. She needs to watch out for a *worm in the apple* when she picks them up from the ground under her apple tree."

Get Up On The Wrong Side Of The Bed

this idiom describes whenever a person gets out of bed in a grouchy mood (and stays that way for the rest of the day)

Example: "Sam stepped in cat urine when he got up this morning. For the rest of the day he was grouchy; like a man who *got up on the wrong side of the bed*."

a derogatory term used to describe someone who is not brave, but cowardly (also known as "chicken")

Example: "Ralph was too frightened to move. The commander called him a   ."

You Can't Judge A Book By It's Cover

one cannot judge the quality or character of someone else, or something else, by appearances only

Example: "Dave and Irvin are upset that they didn't pick Shorty for their basketball team. They just found out that he was last year's Slam Dunk King. They learned, the hard way, that *you can't judge a book by it's cover*!"

Zone Out

this idiom describes when a person stops paying attention.... a type of day-dreaming to give the mind a rest

Example: "Our next door neighbor's son is having trouble in his new school. His teacher has reported that he has difficulty paying attention to his school work. 'It seems that the young man prefers to *zone out*, rather than to focus!' she told his parents."

CPSIA information can be obtained
at www.ICGtesting.com
Printed in the USA
BVHW010458231121
622231BV00007B/204

9 781088 006580